If suppose we are a fragment

If suppose we are a fragment

rob mclennan

BuschekBooks

Ottawa

Library and Archives Canada Cataloguing in Publication

McLennan, Rob, 1970-, author
     If suppose we are a fragment / by rob mclennan.

Poems.
ISBN 978-1-894543-81-1 (pbk.)

     I. Title.

PS8575.L4586I85 2014   C811'.54   C2014-902708-7

Cover image: Untitled [detail] 30" x 30" acrylic on canvas
by Felix Berube

Printed in Winnipeg, Manitoba, Canada by Hignell Book
Printing.

BuschekBooks
P.O. Box 74053
5 Beechwood Avenue
Ottawa, Ontario, Canada K1M 2H9
www.buschekbooks.com

say what you will but what about the land
lady he rents his words from
     Dennis Cooley, "what of the woman who recedes"

We write only of mutual love, Yunshi says.

Mutual as a dream of yourself in a barrel
headed over Niagara.

Love is more singular than mutual.
More a windowpane so clear that birds

sail right through it.
     bianca stone, *someone else's wedding vows*

The new physics gives us no comfort. It diluted the matter,
but burdened the light.
     Leonardo Sinisgalli, trans. Brendan Hennessey,
     "The Poet Forgets What He Has Written," *Sentence* 6

Table of contents:

If suppose we are a fragment

If suppose we are a fragment,

I address you in
phrases, not

in sentences; impatience,
without form,

a hard line sand
is drawn,

     what?
go deep, neighbour;
snow flies,

blends; we get the
real stuff,

damn you; absence,
upholstery,

delights
in pale clothed bodies,

    , container,
resistance, triumph; constant,
& hidden,

   this boundary
we hold up; one-sided,
since,

C.

Achilles himself cannot wish
to slay himself for the wrong
he has done to his alter-ego Hector
Hector disguised as Patroclus
Hector self-object of Achilles
Who by impersonating Achilles
will ever overtake the tortoise
          Susan Howe, *Pierce-Arrow*

Words; explain
in pearled segments

                , a hearty sense
                of explanation

dream of outside; boots & waking,
slippery, rubber soles

we stretched by, here;
above all others

                great historic; silhouette
                of similar thought,

                slate by a
                collapsed window,

designed by deed
& yielding, done

                widow font; we press on,

Once locked now open, space
of a door,

        these symbols of sadness,
        to turn such angles

        to action, speech; a text,

superstition, fixed skywards,
remake a notebook

        a curved pool beckons,
        unremarked,

        curled, centre,

how is it you could stand
in such a shallow, porcelain dish

of tepid water,
eyes closed

explaining moisture away?

No sky; the colours
evidence,

a ring road; half a black eye,
don't, red turn,

no matter how; resurface,
surface, blacktop, gravel

black heart, heart

does not keep
windsong; hill a feed

once tilted,
tilt

a river gone past snow
or stockyard,

An umbrella's acceptance
of surfaces,

> black rain,
> rain

lost temperate seasons, books
sleep, acres of

> ; windshorn,
> a coffee cup

once a brand-new intern; caress,
you make this

, bearable; a sledge
of sentimental care

> a lot of people talk,
> are talking

cut through a cart of light,

> what is it they say?

No evidence of things
but things,

could not take back,

mess of tables,
a promise of thickets,

stop listening to landlords,
November rain is cold,

is coldest yet,

handle carefully; compress
the heart-stone,

pulled, tight; crushed
under impossible storms,

thick, the endless breach,

Not a postscript
but a new page, turned

blank, and still
be written;

I wanted change
, to not break; narrative,

thick and strange,

syllables; out streetcar pulp
to brandish knives,

recycled cobblestone,

a horoscope
of foreign voyages,

long, and vellum-thin,

Pretend; these words I type
a contract,

      bitter, wing

in distant streets, we live
beyond each limit,

      Laurentian hills,
      gravel cadence, rings

bewildered; swings
a castle slipper

      form neither cause,
      solution,

      is at fault,

breathable; lungs,

Practice, restraint,

for days in bed, through
ventricles

        , milk-fed
        naked

apartment dark as
caves,

        artichoke hearts,

this jawline set
of seasons,

        , bric-a-brac
        or bridgework,

posts a drizzle, mix

This has nothing to do
with anything;

red balloon a strata,
rolling downhill,

crime-fight,

convalescent jeer;

the past invents derivatives,
oblique stem, beginning

of investment;

disappears, at present
; damage

, a damned thing,

Murdered a flush wrong,
thigh, a reckon,

    cracked; dead temperate,

an expert in resizing,
living every word

that emerged from her mouth

    a wavelength; force
    , one day

    enter rooms

sleepily; digital hands
hold hours, down

the hour

    beware wakefulness

    : it spreads,

A tire-tread; all the mental customs,
record keepers,

      , what risked nothing

history: unhooked our losses,
marriages that never

      , threadbare
      caked in ash

a thin bread; wizened ash
and keep, returning failure

      a maze of
      fearful, straight lines,

      push

how to map a changing travelogue,
chart happy, polar depths,

lively in its boots;

Ribcage, middle c
particulates,

, deflates

a conflict, boiled
down to point,

, combined reflection,
pretend,

a spherical notion,
sometimes a great theory

of untuned strings,

turn
, turn

so high above the earth, appears
so small,

Stockyards; shelves
constructed out of tights,

, a master-plan

a bush erupts; chick-pea,
rose petal, figs; eyes

, windshield preserves

what have I lost?
Jack Spicer wrote,

when shall I start to sing?

stop talking; goose is cooked,
glass pie-plate, returned

and almost clean,

cracked sidewalks
, red balloons

Rock-smart, hip
a heavy ember,

, avocado pits
an edge

of many days

wishbone; single-servings
clear, and clear

the lights in human form,

drives; imaginary church
we never glimpsed

in folk-tale woods; we walked,
were folk ourselves,

; thin panic-moon,

Sonnets of poppies; curdles
under breath,

a promise, lesser-than

    , palmed
    was never purchased

brown mixing bowl; would fall to earth,
would feed on pearls,

and constant renovation; bare
but for new paint, layers-spread,

these walls,

    replacing even air,
    the riverbank,

    a cherished

    long address,

A note on capability; being,
rewards,

a windmill we,

> step up; wilted floor,
> articulate,

> titled; sad
> phonetics

have taken mountains; shrouds fall
, bodied, mix

of unnerved hell
and fire,

> swim a slim stream,
> custom,

> elegantly-made,

and covered; safe
amid these hidden structures,

A true story; little lessons,
whistling the wind,

       , a sea-breeze
       cumulus, accumulating,

of course the lights were bright,
the curtain; audience,

somehow given,
Cassandra; miles, in her shoes

a deft stroke; list, and run,

       unmanageable,
       a clear and virgin flight,

sidewalk, I am black,

injurious; unwelcome,

The hardest toil
of bridges,

how many moons
come months; full throttle,

recipes in outer space; whelp,
high reckon,

attraction; I but equal then,

ebb and flow,
the mouth swings

up, along

a time now, we devote

, description; portraiture,

false harmony of bees,

Curtain calls; an unknown word
; experience,

      , trickles
      wrapped up in a bird

may be a matter; I couldn't tell,
spread wing across

a summer's day,

      a favourite mistake,
      pasteurized,

      and scattered,

mark the foreground; turmoil,

      where do these thoughts
      come crashing; pierce

      reflective selves

monologue across a neighbourhood,
a balance made of clocks,

Ribcage; middle c,
a molten metal,

       can't undo; what
       still,

melts, pre-snowfall; satisfied,
so sparse description,

disappear, unseen

       swims, into
       a splendid lake,

       would simmer

you say you love

the spirit, and the thought,
what doesn't return,

       to develop a tendency, towards
       , ambivalence

to understand; I fail,

Bone-hinged; days ease
full across blue,

the symbols, turn,
harsh angles into speech,

a coupon; torn,
and chicken-wire

how taste can chance
and feeling, for

the seasons; fool dime,
stark and quickly spent,

storm exposure,
frozen down to seed,

the vine

how stone and deep lone sailors,
an unrequited Fiddler's Green,

collecting stolen moments

, a human in free fall

Escarpment pages,

Dear other, I address you in sentences.
Kathleen Fraser, *Each Next*

Horizontal borders

On bad days I notice the dwindling field mice, their
pacemaker scars. I don't want garments or social gestures.
Step undressed to the door for the mail. The frozen
particles of holiday muzak, a shadow only in name. I pack
a landscape out of screen doors. Your letters age. On good
days: let the water rush unchallenged in. The pulpy mass of
paper heart becomes. Other notes come in, further afield.
A close-up up pithy molecules. I would understand these
marks. If her lips were shaped as cudgels.

Notation,

Squirrels tear around the foundation, mistaking limpid
nodes. From a distance, seven bridges take seven brothers,
until the colours fade. There are no words. Rain evaporates,
returns to itself. I would like to know what Charles II
discovered about science, the Royal Society, the sake of
telescopes. What he thought he had learned. I want to
know what he saw his investments become. I want to know
if he thought it was worth it.

The note beginning

Score, across a perfect pitch. With the ability of careless
outskirts, bodies of lingering meaning. I would enjoy this.
He writes, there is still daylight in some people. Sublime.
The blood moon fractals, a misbegotten strike-through,
slowly removing cotton garments. In my mind, the eclipse,
the sudden way sentiment overcame, diminished. We
hesitate. The newly dead float past prairie ghost towns, the
St. Lawrence River, and on down the Hudson. You can
wrap your head in the moon, and still. Charred drawings
of little airplanes.

Little sentences,

Each mark is equal to a line or a separate lie. The word
sonnet scratched onto green paper. An envelope edge torn
off as a bookmark. The hair of each curled photo cracks at
the crease, memories that no longer remember. Once you
were gone I divided into two distant pools.

I have a long thought

A book she recommended. How to Paint Charcoal. Spray-painted brush. Against the side of the hair salon machines wear down an orange word. We exhale vignettes. Eyes of a moth that are only painted. As far from the harvest, suddenly remembering someone else's wedding vows. It returned like the worst of security, the taint of a Poor Man's Stew. Whether or not God exists, He wouldn't set foot in here. They say Adam set down at Ararat, deep sunk in stone. No word on whether left or his right, the same number of toes. Everything distracts. I couldn't see past.

The invention of writing

Ingrained, this resistance to struggle. Mathematical points. I repeat the arousal song of her borders, even as I step back. Sometimes I get turned around. Snow squalls, threatening daybreak. Had you ever wondered. Had she. We were marking up hours. Filament of the speed that the brain changes colour. We have not arrived. We are here. An experience of spiders. Saw you last from those uppermost branches. Or was that her. Words trickle down into feeling. New paper we press with first language, our hands.

Hotel Victoria,

You were crossing the bridge with the air from my knee.
Elevated, accurate as a separate morning. I am worse than
you. Better. We were inside obsessions. Interior dread:
darkened hallways, and lamentable wallpaper, softly
embroidered. Every moment a breath, the resurrection of
echo. Your space on the mattress imprints a daguerreotype.
I can see your reflection. These rooms aren't nearly as small
as you have become.

Museum, pieces

I was dreaming a rough patch. Had I too much speed or
touched brake, I'd have lost to the bushes. Artifacts become
temporarily misplaced. They float out of windows. The
central point of the crack isn't breaking. Sleep makes up
much, causes hunger. It takes energy to dream this. Why
not take a picture of what this is and what this also is.

The opposite of poetry,

I never knew approximation. We were always precise. The
invention of trickery, to save time and effort. A poppy,
in stubbly light. Each fool makes a doctor, a trading
ship. I would understand doors, thick and scrupulous.
Reproduced as a corpse. A grape hyacinth. Strawberry
posies.

From major to minor,

Compose a frame for entering the dead. I offered the
evening shade. The conifer. Still. Until now, I hadn't
changed bed-sheets. I was alone in this. A flinch in the air.
Picking flowers. Every sentiment you imagine. Intolerable
moon. We castigate stars, rightly so.

A syntax in orbit,

I was falling to earth, burning candles. Melting wax, and
before that, dancers. You were hooked on the colours:
orange, blue, yellow. The new edge of a now-silent country.
Waters function, terrain. A spice in the air stinging eyes.
The changing shapes of the flame. Someone called out,
offstage. Perhaps, the wings.

A terrible decay,

Interchangeable, the air of a small net, like a double bass.
We gut the strings, breathe out light, reflecting through
the waves. A girl dreaming of a muscle, dark. Why must I
leave behind? The history a storm hovers above, alternately
appearing / disappearing. We might bend, but in new
forms. Why must I leave? Make that what.

Linden lea

For tonight I am a window
in a cottage by the sea.
Monica Youn, *Ignatz*

Linden lea,

Betrayed itself a claimant,
once a village,
                    as were all,
escarpment; store-stretch,

lolling clouds; a stream of flags,
step, one step,
                    swans once,
; said, louder,

          do you know history,
a river ran, utterance a dead
, split upward,
                    past the stones
of our assembling,

A door is closed, closed

Metric is wasted time; a lavender room
                can slightly blue, if sun sits;
what occurs

when the position comes? your empty calm in needs,
white broach of window, blank,
        silver razor crossing undershirt,

river calls a door, a second storey,
what saved,
      we eat by, hand,

rich harbour, sentenced; carbides,

wet embankment, shiver; dog scurries in
                  & hurriedly, slips,

Doctors without borders,

An allied craft,
, dependent

      , no such thing,
a neighbourhood breathes & breeds,
waits, standing

on the corner; uniforms,
plates license-red, the piercings
      of barista nose & navel,

what do you see
against suspicion; red wheelbarrows,
chickens & a fatal wound,

the boy will live; he has to,

An impulse of weather,

Such great heights; nocturnal,
this creaking century
, rattles on; abound,

, direction, this and miss,
hit and turn; a simple drive,

tells the hour mark; the eldest,
tin type page

                        , a meditation long on glass
in waves; spells only water out, alight

these sheets through windowshine,
, direct; opposition,

Ghazal for Rideau Terrace,

A stretch of horse the day
could only muster,

terrible in places; ambulatory,

neighbours remark; hardly
a consistent stretch,

dog park howls; hours
the package grows,

what sleeping planets orbit, spread

some wrong is done; avenged
a tongue skin silky porcelain,

front step to porch; descends,

The glimmer of wing,

Understood, the metal bowl of song
unsung,
                    gone, canary, under
corpulent; this sharp fold

rises, overhang & hold, the bottle

        , substituting body parts,
a jealous individual
is nothing to discuss;
                    , because

you were, once, a stranger; go west,
down, until the ocean strikes,

bested by a thought,

That expression of the indefinite,

Grey afternoon that hangs held breath,
gesture of a damp,
                              , signature
, green shutters you could touch
            , attention, not the body

late development, subdivide the core
to the highest degree of burning,
            , phosphorescent light

as guilty as you; a deck no longer,
shovels, snow, a scream
                              , comes down as sparks,

Arrow, with a rope attached,

The end of weight; a wanting,
wanted more, a glass shard, scar
　　　　, the origins of nothing, more

adept at this, in breathing, held
　　　　throughout an afternoon of liquid,

first meetings; at the bar; explosive
　　　　　　　　　, plastic organs,
reflections, as in
non-reflective polish; dense glossy clusters,
　　　　slept; a border

of diminutive suns; I swear I saw this,
glaze & dawn & breaks,

　　　　, picturesque architecture, mature trees
　　　　　　　　& plentiful green,

drifting sugar in compressed air;

Crazy daisies, & wooden stars,

Endured, if since past infancy,
she touches my face; the linens
        , to see such awe,

worked in relation to the contrary,

        , what if we'd been shaped?
an accurate point; the falling here
or down, there
                        , vertical

, gnawing; drown a small mass,
        , grief a soft spot; wasted,

More abrupt, than

Each sinner, left; an arch of nose,
what you believe; a noose,
      sometimes

               , provocative, a scale
or circuit-breaker; swims out, Olympic,
terror-skilled a system etched
     , in sideways; drink up,

because the sidewalks are sepia,

    , the boundaries of
dynamic affirmation, paint-wheels,
montage of illusions, optic
         & Cyrillic,

credible, &
    a little vague,

Assembled into a long dialogue,

The thinking world & thinking of; adept,
uncertain as a something,
                                        sun
            gone yellow-white to green,

make copies, please; a hyphen-face is lifted,
snow drifts & a dollop,
                              where
            do we address these limits,
            margins?

component streets, enclave
of so few cars,
                        a bowling green,
goes on to say; before this,
grow & swimming melt; with cold hands,
            rush all,
                              in one place; stones,

Between an x & y,

Drowning down, a; star-shaped hour, rich
one-hundred fold,
a spate of pharmacies; the image
of each afternoon;

the naked face; they say the universe is curved,

land, water, air; the earliest movies
, extensions of hewn glass, stone leading
variations on stone,

we have people who listen,
have children,
have not;
Paul Anka sings;

a midday glare of clouds; we chart the names of dogs,

Boulevard,

Slippage; central points & white swans,
        , feathers we shoulder;
                        Beechwood Cemetery Road,
Rockcliffe wind; a boy shifts in his chair

but keeps staring out the window; to sudden such,

                , cracks, in which; blank,
days of error; misbegotten, strike-through,
narratives in tapestry,

off-base & strong; a dream
of separate storeys, hallways long,
                        that little place where echoes
        drop, inside,

the snow is pure & pure & driven; she,

Marginalia,

Writ in, from Maple Lane, scratch
Beechwood, estates articulate,

      , marked & carved, yard-thick,
constructed out of nervous fragments,

less urgent, language
burned from a name, a playground,
          , parking lot,

      orange peels; cut loose; out seeking
where
the dead live,

The sun upon this, skin

Once wounded, hounds; wooly hats
             so complement the eyes; expressive,

; the other side / a plain French door,

      , amid   , the black slant
                               of euphoria,

safely; unspeakable acts, of azure script
pictured purple thistle, beheld

      , in vellum; blood more red,

old movie reels address, in kind,
a supernatural edge,

of content; the image of the fingers, hand

We see not only,

So bitter, froze; the floodwaste,
                    , swears the birds were, wintered,
mint & minted; photographs,

what seems to waver; downturn,
            everything a grain; white wash,

the trees of meaning; mouth of iron,
skin mineral-soft, a port of rich vein,
            wealthy shallows bred,

the world, incorporating form,
less perfect squares, as lining up
                    as object, near

a plane that hums in, hitch

am needing, proof; same clothes as the previous,

Talking points,

The charm, of Adams' garden
, suburb style; hunched body holding
                    , snowplow, shovel, scrape
the base bare down to

            , heart; how once you hovered,
deep blue slope of designate, a speech; wings
                        an ever formal, ornamental
in design;
                    scone posters; Queen Victoria
in Queen Anne's lace, the difference
, cursive elbows, fabric-thin,
            rowing through the centre of a story,

expressive watercolours; a life
pulled at from corners,

companion at your heels,

too far from shore to notice, matter;

Lost, & then found

In the never order, correct; lost, lost
& lost; the hand gives up the writing; conducts
                          , a loss in floodplains

to speak in music, peace, in plain,
right-angle view-finds
                          , out a city window
looks light out the corner; turns,

an apparition of my thoughts an arm
, length
            , what at stake, here; sympathies,
especially a fire,
dedicated,
                        , earlier, a some
are cast in different lapses,

            you lost, little girl,
            , your mother,
            mother,

seen addressed as such; a coin,

Sub-division,

years sentenced to wander
were lodged outside the city for fear of
            Cole Swensen, *Such Rich Hour*

Old farmers, field

Side entrance to lilacs, trees fenced in,
walk us at noon, last seen
       , pavement; courtesy of expansion,

outstanding, in the field; or winded,

broken window cafe plights
a growth spurt; bookstore leaves
       , could go with houses, petrified,
she tries her tongue a crude,

whole, enduring salvage; the records
show, that; heritage of undefined,
                    in special projects
       , folder focus evidence a folding, in

or cut up, carve, disjunct, divorce, a parting
                , severance,

collectible, proliferate; she recommends
                  , you punch out stars
      , some good advice;

Suburban aria,

A mist of, fills the lungs; bruised clouds
         kept in motion; commercial jets that lift,

against the windy grain; an opera house
                  of yellow company,

queen of quick-fast; sell me
your love,

what beauty left left me in rags; fathom
of a pressure, when

             , intestines rupture, break
, re-colonize; left in song,

scrubbed off your machine; a dusty
breeze,
           , a painting of John Lennon
& Santa Claus is just,
               , confusing

Calcium deposit,

Cipher; grey & bitter,
                  looking down; beloved litany, a twitter
, that which I have not,

a shelf-life in Vancouver; crossed over
        Sapper's Bridge
                  , unpleasant over; insisting, out of sleeves,

remained, insistent; everything remains,

a corpse of lodge pines, conifers, what
                  , of leaving, realized,
my understanding; complex,

the last of which Longinus said,

portrait of a soft space, writing
                  , stairway lying on his back, forever

Cul-de-sac,

Can you say what matters; equestrian,
                   a slate of wartime starlets, actors,
develop a new star; harbour
            in this witness,

banish from fence-lines; a second
of profound encounters; starlings, crows, a
            hundred thousand,
air currents swirl, pool tidal,

fabulous; assembled here,

into Prague, a march of hens
& syntax; grave
         in unexpected ways,

mall-adjacent; call me when you disappear,

12 untitled and unknown coordinates,
epyllions,
, epithelials

Sentences fell apart but they had always been a
part.

Brenda Hillman, *Practical Water*

`The possibilities of love poems
in a time of prosody,

or perhaps only foolishness,

the paint takes time to dry

the briefest Saskatchewan,
a fickle & furtive,

brown snow slush as pure

to paint over a smell doesn't mask
or remove

but permanently bond

slip a quarter heart quarter a payphone

the fear of receiving love
, unsure what to do with it

a noun is not alphabet you
break like a word

are you not pure

not a morning enough to contain,

A terrible journey of tenses,
how do you did,

rhythm of tongues & of tongue,
the beast needs more torque,

the slow future of crosswords

learned to write in cold bedrooms
of airplanes & knives

a warm kitchen of cadence

you make efforts to modernize,

I look up from my reading,
stranger pushes the pull door

unhinged from the orchard
of whispers,

winter bodies

the morning itself claims permission
to talk through the arrangements,

The mad glare of spectacle,

dance under the eaves, the old woman
banned from the Second Cup,

who isn't that old

sideways, cellphone slip

prone to know, three police cruisers
no epic contains,

a description enough to forget,

Carling Avenue, Preston, polling citizens
to step storeys up, bodes,

the past is sometimes
more than foreign, a new

-ly discovered genus,

architectural purge,

strip the pulpy heart like an apple,
toss the unbroken peel

wait for it to land

in the shape of initial,
the last woman who broke you

I have no province,

hands out,
forgive

waveforms, carved bovine flesh,
a service of cells

the watchful molecular eye
morning light gathers strength,

& returns,

the hour your January car needed
to thaw, melt

down icy slopes,

sick of the wait

renewable as canopy, sequins, panoptic
of stars,

out of vocabulary, rivers of drink,
explosive in parts

ignition filled gasping breath
& myths of pure origin,

baseball love a transistor-head, doubled

a key turns, repeat, over,

Rain water for sparrows

secret language of yellows, of reds,
pretty colonies, lined

lisp, he marks, epithodes,

there was little to keep
in the nakedness,

Winchester warm,

your heartbeat returned me to earth

I am reading you under the maple,
fixing once to record

the back of the throat, in still
human trills,

rolling tones, gather
no consonants, moss

the world left & I felt

the present held under the water
the present held under the water

leaves us no spaces, air

Hearts require a future
to hang,

held, not a hook

atmosphere of perennials,

sentences remake in walled cities,
a century withers

sparrow's corpse rests on the cold
soft shoulder,

suburb of snowy children, & cool
rainy women,

the stone soup of men,

the storm that surrendered
once into first light,

the problem with hiding is,

where St. Adele, a worn map
verbed across blue horizon,

less a matter of hyphens,

Soft heart of ash, fragment

the floor model of absolute sincerity
test worn,

abandoned,

fibres knew in the seat cushion,
rested, in pairs

we forget how to fly,

I anoint myself place-marker,
ashamed,

the wind tore through the brush
& the tear,

& untended brush,

what is this fear dressed in satin,

understood to be frightening
poems of tens, thens

the moon full above parking lots,
all else is cloud

Were her legs scissors
or kitchen knives, twinned

I haven't the patience for

a tea made from lemon
& ginger

my mind what you mind changes nothing

dark matter made ornamental
with irony,

work months that reduce down,
past zero

a space made of nothing

adrift in the echo of things,
its only citizen

a space marked in the earth
does not rest between it

sweet mouth, holding second degree burns,

this whisper of blue,

Rommell drives deep,
we are dying, Egypt, echoes, the troops

push a surge,

assist me, good friends

ice approached the canal, sleeps
in past freedoms,

& present smooth surfaces,

is this carrying description,
a parcel

hands outline a shadow

a government that forms
on strategies, polls

not ideas, or ideals

the backdrop of new buildings,
an artificial lake

playback loons through the mist,

faded, you promised me
windmills to tilt,

A desired politician, falls away
over time,

skin samples, white pine,
depictions of angels

explorations of tides,
what presence the moon makes

abandon desire,
develop habits instead,

the smell of you that was different

the telephone, sits
at an angle,

rueful Ottawa cold,
pure pleasure

my lungs made,

trace of skin from the palm,
deliberately scratched

a scar, of some surfaces

lighter,

Would you limit the silence,
profane undertones

the usual
obligations,

made tablets, construction & mystery,

a pine forms visible trace
in the heavens

a spectacle of bare cheekbones,
of weightless array

tied my fortune to ice-caps

beyond autumn's spectacle
, breaking bonds

molecular bridge,
the dry riverbed lyric

in the crosshairs of colour, some gender

decades of warm wind, of growth,
a test of the senses

a wavelength brought calm,

a special
abstract of lines, cleared & cut

This withering heat

I no longer recall,
twenty below in the shade,

an hourglass resting on side
makes twin pools,

sentences broaden, through spillage

the mark of a breath of a breath
of an hour,

fingers the daylight made nothing of

to limit by naming,
you called it,

violin bow salvaged from underneath chairs,
I watched him retrieve,

quite distinct,
watermark stamp,

awake in high-heels, picture perfect,
you step into the shower

burst of burnt sun over Chinatown,
Royal Arch

forms an error,

Acknowledgments:

Some of these have appeared previously in print and/
or online in *Acta Victoriana* (Toronto ON), BlazeVOX
(Buffalo NY), *The Capilano Review* (Vancouver BC), *The
Dusty Owl Quarterly Vols. 27-42* (Ottawa ON), *Handsome
Journal* (Boston MA), *Softblow* (Singapore), *Sunfish: Poetry
Magazine* (Manchester England), one of Richard Hansen's
poems-for-all chapbooks, *Museum, pieces* (Sacramento CA:
Series #1062), and as an above/ground press pamphlet for
the annual *Peter F. Yacht Club* Christmas party/reading/
regatta at the Carleton Tavern, Thursday, December 30,
2010.

The section "Linden lea" appeared as a chapbook through
Jordan Fry and Priscilla Brett's Grey Borders (Niagara
Falls ON), produced in June 2011 as part of their first
annual Niagara Literary Arts Festival; "Escarpment pages,"
appeared as a chapbook in June 2011 through Rupert
Loydell's smallmindedbooks (Exeter, England), and again,
in February 2012 through Apostrophe Press (Ottawa ON),
for the sake of adventures in and around New Orleans with
Stephen Brockwell and Marthe Reed; and the poem "C"
appeared as a chapbook in summer 2011 through Dawn
Pendergast's little red leaves (Houston TX). Thanks so
much to all the editors and publishers involved.

The sequence "C." alters, borrows and steals phrases from,
as well as responding to, Christine McNair's *Evidence*
(Ottawa ON: cartywheel press, 2010). The sequence
"12 untitled and unknown coordinates, / epyllions, / ,
epithelials" reacts and responds to Brenda Hillman's *Pieces
of Air in the Epic* (Middletown CT: Wesleyan, 2005) and

Practical Water (Middletown CT: Wesleyan, 2009), and appeared as both print and e-chapbook in February 2012 with Free Poetry For.

Part of this was written in Ottawa's Lindenlea neighbourhood, during a mid-January house-sit for Stephen Brockwell, in the shadow of the painting which graces the cover. *Thanks* for that, sir.

Thanks, too, to Felix Berube for permission to reproduce his artwork on the cover, and to Camille Martin and Cole Swensen for their ongoing generosities.

This book is for Christine McNair.

November 2010— January 2011
Ottawa

Author's Biography

Born in Ottawa, Canada's glorious capital city, rob mclennan currently lives in Ottawa. The author of nearly three dozen trade books of poetry, fiction and non-fiction, he won the CAA/Air Canada Prize in 1999, the John Newlove Poetry Award in 2010, the Council for the Arts in Ottawa Mid-Career Artist Award in 2014, and was longlisted for the CBC Poetry Prize in 2013. His most recent titles include *The Uncertainty Principle: stories*, (2014), a second collection of essays, *Notes and dispatches: essays* (2014), and a second novel, *missing persons* (2009). His poetry, fiction and critical work has appeared in over two hundred publications worldwide, including *Open Letter, The Globe & Mail, Jacket2, Rain Taxi, RAMPIKE, Prairie Fire, New American Writing, The Antigonish Review, filling Station, Arc Poetry Magazine, Numéro Cinq, The Capilano Review, Literary Review of Canada, The Colorado Review, American Letters & Commentary* and *The Poetic Front*, and he has been a regular columnist for *Open Book: Ontario* since 2009. An editor and publisher since 1993, he runs above/ground press, Chaudiere Books (with Christine McNair), *seventeen seconds: a journal of poetry and poetics* (ottawater.com/seventeenseconds), *Touch the Donkey* (touchthedonkey.blogspot.com) and the Ottawa poetry pdf annual *ottawater* (ottawater.com). He spent the 2007-8 academic year in Edmonton as writer-in-residence at the University of Alberta, and regularly posts reviews, essays, interviews and other notices at robmclennan.blogspot.com

Also by the author

poetry

Songs for little sleep,
grief notes:
A (short) history of l.
apertures
Glengarry
kate street
52 flowers (or, a perth edge)--essay on phil hall--
wild horses
a compact of words
gifts
solids, or, strike-out (a suite)
The Ottawa City Project
aubade
name   , an errant
stone, book one
what's left
red earth
paper hotel
harvest, a book of signifiers
bagne, or Criteria for Heaven
The Richard Brautigan Ahhhhhhhhhhh
Manitoba highway map
bury me deep in the green wood
Notes on drowning

fiction

The Uncertainty Principle: stories,
missing persons
white

non-fiction

Notes and Dispatches: essays
Alberta Dispatch: interviews & writing from Edmonton
Ottawa: The Unknown City
subverting the lyric: essays